JAIL 101
Things to Know When *You* Go!

Friedman Newman

© 2007 Todd Russo
© 2010 Chris Kelsey
All Rights Reserved.

No part of this publication may be reproduced, stored in a retrieval system, or transmitted, in any form or by any means, electronic, mechanical, photo-copying, recording, or otherwise, without the written permission of the author.

This book is printed on acid-free paper.

Printed in the United States of America

Table of Contents

Foreword

1. Dress Warm
3. Sex
5. Weapons "Tooth Brush Sword" and "Fecal Flyer"
9. Lose weight: "Feel Great"
11. Masturbation
13. Phone Calls
15. Bail
17. Public Defender vs. Private Attorney
19. Riots
21. Panic Button "Room Service"
23. Crying
25. Escape
27. Clothing
29. Handcuffs
31. Letters
33. Hard Drugs
35. Smoking
37. Apologizing
39. Self Defense
41. Time Management
43. "Fifi Bags"
45. Trumped up Charges "Are You Serious?"
49. Jail Etiquette
53. Profanity
55. Suicide
57. Bunks
59. Toilet Use
61. Quest For Fire
63. Jail Lingo
65. Commissary

- 67. Snitching
- 69. Gangs
- 71. Spork
- 73. Address Concealment
- 75. H_2O Through A Door
- 77. Chow Times
- 79. Hygiene
- 81. Grievance Forms
- 83. Journals "Chronicle Your Incarceration"
- 87. Routines
- 91. Credit For Time Served "Be Good And Get Out Early"
- 93. Visits
- 95. Jail House Lawyers "Good Advice Is Easy To Find"
- 97. Religion "Soul Food"
- 99. Shower Shots "Wear Your Shower Shoes"
- 101. Latex Pillows
- 103. Pardons and Programs "P. S. P."
- 107. Jail Dentistry "Extractions Happen"
- 109. Simple Flatulence
- 111. Conduct
- 115. Hanging Feet "Please Don't Manson Me!"
- 117. Jail Cuisine "Meals Petite"
- 121. Jail Juice "Ring In The Holidays Or Just Get Gaveled"
- 123. Know Thy Captors
- 124. "Stronger Each Day"

Sabrina,

A safe harbor have you been,
during my life's all too frequent storms.
Your beauty, generosity, and kindness grace us all.

Thank you

FOREWORD

Approximately 500 people will be struck by lightning in the United States this year. In the same annual period, approximately 14,000,000 people will be arrested.

For the first time in the history of America, more than 1 in 100 adults is behind bars. Based on 2008 "Bureau of Justice Statistics", one's ethnicity weighs heavily into the likelihood of being incarcerated; the highest rate being 1 of every 15 Black men 18 or older. Hispanic men 18 or older, rate second, at 1 in every 36; followed by 1 in every 106 White men over 18 years of age. As of this writing, your odds of winning the Mega Millions Jackpot are approximately 1 in 176,000,000.
As of year end 2008, a record 2.3 million people were incarcerated in Federal and State Prisons, or local Jails. This book, written by experienced "scoff-laws", sheds light on what to expect, when they "cuff and stuff" **YOU**.

DRESS WARM

When initially arrested; expect to spend 12-36 hours in less than ideal climes, as you endure being transferred from one bone chilling holding cell to another. This maddening cell shuffle culminates with a "Classification" interview. The "Classification" interview determines where you will be "housed". Example: If you are suspected of misdemeanor D.U.I.; you will typically be placed with other alleged misdemeanor offenders. Similarly, if you are suspected of committing a violent offense, (Armed Robbery, Assault, Homicide, etc.) you will be placed with a collection of much less boring folks. During the initial musical cell dance, do not expect any sympathy from the Deputies or Correctional Officers regarding your near hypothermic condition. Instead; even on the hottest days of August, carry warm clothes, and at the first sign of Police contact, **don** everything you have! At the Jail; your less than comfort conscious hosts, will often times assist you in removing some layers. With this in mind; wisely arm yourself with a bottom layer consisting of a hooded sweatshirt, sweatpants, socks, and always wear shoes. Boots seem like a good idea. However, your new found clothing consultants may believe it gives you an unfair advantage over your "Comrades in cold".

JAIL 101

THINGS TO KNOW WHEN YOU GO

SEX

The creator of this book is a devout heterosexual and the lack of gender mixing at Punitive Institutions presents a fatal impediment to his sexual activity. Jail is not a romantic place for most and even as a homosexual your options are limited. During your initial "Classification" interview; you will be asked if you are a homosexual. Say "yes" and you will be placed with other "poo-jabbers", "cock wranglers", and "rump rangers". This may seem fun at the time. However, the placement of yourself in what is known as "Protective Custody" (P.C.), will be documented and readily available to other inmates who may not share your zeal for alternative lifestyles.

JAIL 101

WEAPONS

Weapons; like inmates, come in various shapes and sizes. Some, such as pencils, are usable in their nascent state. Others, such as our personal favorite, the "toothbrush sword" require some fabrication. To arm yourself with this "dental dagger", proceed as follows: 1. Locate an extra toothbrush. (Do not use your own, dental hygiene is important!) 2. Find a secluded area, away from prying eyes. (Not difficult, considering you are most likely in an 8'x10' cell for 21-24 hours per day) 3. Find an abrasive surface to grind on; another easy task. 4. Hold the bristle end and reshape the handle to a point. Although Correctional Facilities do not issue full length toothbrushes, you will none the less, be armed with an easily concealed, and (think temple, eye, neck, ear) potentially lethal weapon.

JAIL 101

The "Fecal Flyer" is quite simply, the most repulsive long-range instrument of severe illness or death, available to you! It is not a toy and should only be used in a "Custards last stand" situation. In the event, you are identified as the "shooter"; expect to be targeted for death! 1. Start by locating a staple, shard of razor, or other piece of sharp metal. (Use caution: re: razors. Most facilities document there issuance, and frown on there less than intact return) 2. Wrap the staple or razor shard in wet toilet paper, leaving a bit exposed; picture a "spit wad" with a piece of metal protruding from it. The general consensus is for greater control; never exceed ¼ inch in diameter. 3. Create a firing tube. The easiest thing to use would be plastic ink pen housing. However, these do not exist in jail, hence, a time of improvisation is nigh. Roll a piece of magazine, cardboard or book cover into a cylindrical tube. Size the tube to accommodate your projectile. This brings up a valuable point. Always keep whatever adhesive you may find; fruit labels, special meal labels, postage stickers..., anything that sticks, should be kept and concealed of course; keep in mind that the definition of "contraband" becomes broader each day. Use the adhesive sources to secure your firing tube. This is not a "Tommy Gun". You have one shot and your aim cannot be compromised by a less than stalwart "air cannon" 4. Once you have the "spike wad" and "air cannon" prepared, its time for some practice shots. Thanks to social budget cuts, there are many mentally ill "moving targets" in jail. These "knuckle draggers" barely notice and have no way of explaining to authorities that they have been "spiked". 5. After boosting your confidence by many (unfecaled) successful covert launches and contacts to the head and neck. Its time to add the fecal matter! This is where the fun starts. First, let's recap! The goal of this endeavor is to introduce feces into the bloodstream of the targeted organism. Everybody's feces contains E.Coli and a host of other lethal bacteria. Don't argue over whose feces is more deadly, any dollop will do! It's up to you how you obtain and apply the feces to the spike wad, just get it on there. 6. Fire when ready! (CAUTION: Do not inhale the feces bathed "spike wad" into your mouth!)

JAIL 101

LOSE WEIGHT

Have you been putting off shedding a few pounds? Going to jail is your golden opportunity to become a lean and mean incarcerated machine. The RDA was developed in something like... 1958? ("Were criminals, not historians!") And the "chow" offered in jail, just barely grazes those archaic caloric guidelines. In the absence of additional calories via "commissary"; you should have no trouble surpassing even the wildest expectations of that "Jay Craig" lady.

JAIL 101

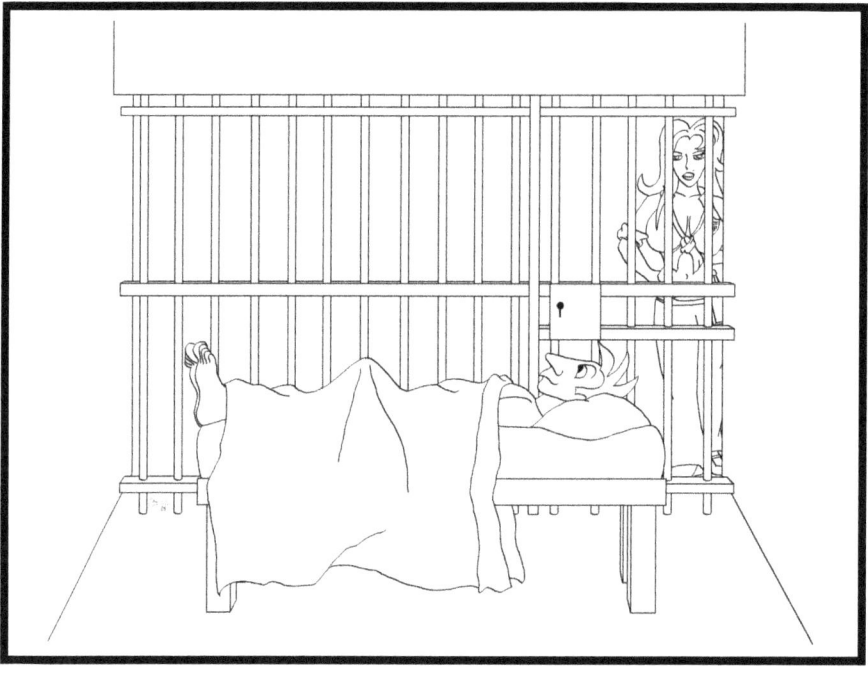

MASTURBATION

Natural urges are stifled for most, by Jails less than romantic ambience. At times however; fortune may smile on you in the form of an opposite sexed Correctional Officer. Periodic late night "walk-throughs", allow you an opportunity to hold court with these eager eyed, jumpsuit clad, closet voyeurs. Use caution: Making eye contact while in the throes of self pleasure, is a.k.a. "Indecent Exposure" or "Lewd Conduct", both misdemeanors.

JAIL 101

PHONE CALLS

You have the right to a phone call from jail. However, these calls "may be monitored and recorded", thereby eliminating the chance of conveying names and addresses of witnesses who need be absent at future court proceedings. Mail is a safer alternative for "hit" arrangements. Phone cards are available from "Commissary". (See "Commissary" section) Note: It may take weeks to get into the "Commissary" loop. So always carry a fully charged, phone card number in your cerebral rolodex, if you lack friends willing to shoulder collect calls.

JAIL 101

BAIL

Bail; a false sense of exoneration, is available for a price; barring a history of F.T.A. (Failure to appear), or being suspected of committing an especially heinous offense. Be selective when "bailing out". The 5-10% given to the bail bondsman is non-refundable. Example: You are being held on an "Assault With A Deadly Weapon" charge (a personal favorite). Depending on how successful the assault was, your bail could range from $25,000 to $100,000. This equates to $2,500 or $10,000 "lost"; half of that if you are a good negotiator. And most likely a co-signer; someone willing to lose their house, if you do not show up for court. Explore International flight options, if you foresee undesirable results in court.

JAIL 101

PUBLIC DEFENDER VS. PRIVATE ATTORNEY

Attorneys are not created equal. Chances are, if you have deep pockets; you will eagerly drop absurd amounts of cash on a "big ad" Lawyer. Unfortunately, this may not enhance your chances of speedy and unhindered (e.g., probation, interlock alcohol devices, restraining orders, inability to buy and possess firearms, etc.) societal re-introduction. Judging by our own experience; Private Attorneys referred by experienced criminals can be trusted to take an interest in something other than their Cayman Islands account. Public Defenders receive salary pay from the State and the amount of energy applied to your quandary may fluctuate wildly. Many Public Defenders work very hard. Other Public Defenders, seem only interested in assisting the D.A. ("Diabolical Asshole") in padding their conviction percentage. Choose wisely and ask for a "continuance" (time to find new Counsel) at the first sign of any collusion with the D.A..

JAIL 101

RIOTS

Riots are easy to predict in most cases. Usually, the normal tempo of the facility will be altered prior to the onset of any bloodletting. If you have foreknowledge and nobody to maim or murder, seek solitude. If the riot is a byproduct of gang warfare and you have pledged allegiance to a warring faction, your participation is obligatory. After regaining control of the facility. The Correctional Officers search for combatants by disrobing (The C.O.'s seem to enjoy this a little too much) everyone and checking for scratches, bruises, stab wounds, and other telltale signs of participation. Unfortunately, full scale prisoner uprisings that catalyze gangs in an effort to overthrow Institutions are rare, but should be joined with joy.

JAIL 101

PANIC BUTTON

In most contemporary "Pod" type jails, there is a button located near the cell door. This button should NOT be pushed unless you have a situation requiring emergency medical assistance or something equally apocalyptic. Example: You are pinned by "Bolo the bunghole banger" Once pushed, this button activates a siren and light outside your door, making it impossible to deny responsibility. The Respondents to your issue, clad in steel toe boots, will no doubt, not appreciate the gravity of anything less than assault or death, and likely replicate a scene from "A Clockwork Orange", with you as the horizontal main attraction.

JAIL 101

CRYING

At some point during your stay, you may find yourself less than enthusiastic or even depressed. These emotional states may lead to a physiological reaction known as "crying". Prisoners and Correctional Officers, both a hardened lot, are not especially sympathetic to your spectrum of emotions. At minimum, much like Grammar School, you will be ridiculed. However, because this is Jail, you may also end up being labeled a "bitch", and end up with your "end up". Reserve all crying for late at night, in your bunk, under the covers, and never, ever sob! Tears only!

JAIL 101

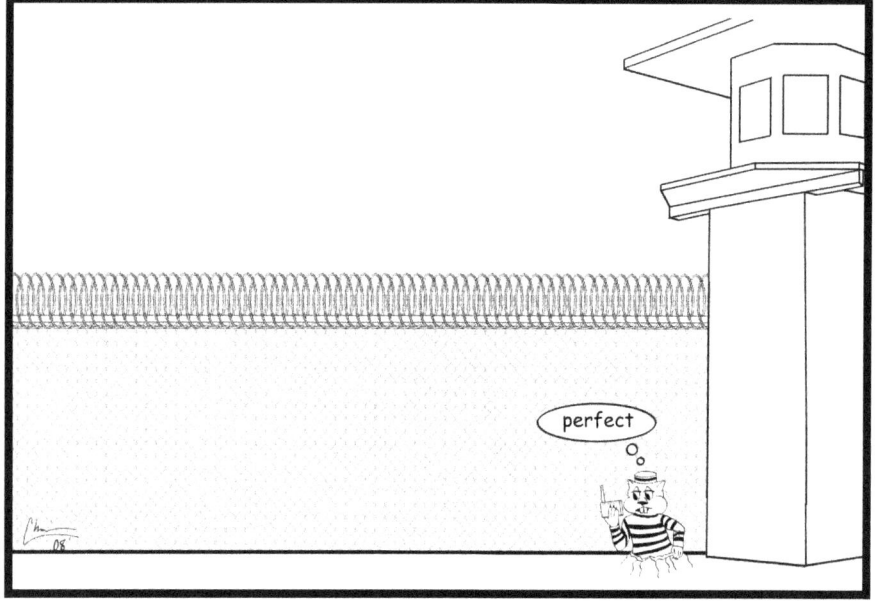

ESCAPE

Additional time granted for escape attempts ranges from thirty days to five years. Carefully consider the repercussions of a failure before plotting, planning, or engaging in knee-jerk sprinting, for unapproved liberty. If you have three weeks remaining of your sentence, you may just want to ride it out. On the other hand, if you have an excessive amount (2-20 years) of time remaining; what the hell, give it a shot! Help is always necessary. Seek like minded individuals (easy to find), and finely tune the details to insure yourself a 95% chance of success before launching. There are countless ways to escape and countless ways for your attempt to be foiled. We will not itemize them here. However, we will provide you with our personal favorite, The "Techno-Gopher". The main impediment in the initiation of the "Techno-gopher" escape plan, is the acquisition of a G.P.S. device. You must find someone willing to "Keester" it in. (Good luck!) After you've cleaned up the G.P.S. device, its time to go for a walk. Look for a place with soft soil, away from prying eyes. Once located, mark the coordinates. Next: Send the location to your friends outside, and have them secure a private residence as proximal as possible. This may prove to be burdensome and expensive, so have them consider alternatives, such as "Home Invasion". Very little guesswork is involved in the remaining facets of "Techno-Gopher" release process. Your co-conspiring friends simply tunnel to the location given, and you burrow to freedom when timely.

JAIL 101

CLOTHING

Each facility has a unique taste in fashion. Some prefer orange, some prefer green, others prefer blue or even brown. Whatever their choice, it is obligatory you follow suit, and do not be surprised by their lack of interest in seasonal guidelines!

JAIL 101

HANDCUFFS

Handcuffs are restricting and allow little room for self expression. The days of "Houdiniing" your way out of them are over, due to advanced locks and keys. As a rule, the less you struggle during the application process, the less inclined the applicator (Correctional or Police Officer) will be to "cinch off" any hopes of circulation to your hands. At times, you may feel uncomfortable wearing this type of "Heavy jewelry", behind your back. To move them to the front: simply sit down, pull your legs through and "wah la" they will be in front! Caution: Your hosts may not appreciate your dexterity and exhibit their disapproval by (you guessed it!) replicating a scene from "A Clockwork Orange".

JAIL 101

LETTERS

Letters from loved ones are a critical component in the maintenance of your morale. However: All incoming mail is judiciously searched, and depending on the nature of the contraband, the sender may be arrested. Use false return addresses for "Shower shots", etc. Outgoing letters are not opened and should be X-rated whenever possible to promote your "Criminal Cretin" identity.

HARD DRUGS

Hard drugs are available in jail. Some are brought in by Correctional Officers. Most are brought in by Inmates on short stays, such as, "Weekenders" or Work Furlough Prisoners ("I'm not snitching, this is common knowledge!"). Most of these Prisoners endure "strip searches", so the majority of the drugs are smuggled inside the "Mules" body. Some swallow the heroin, methamphetamine, cocaine, or crack, wrapped in balloons or condoms. A day or two later the "Mule" and their "Friends", or is that "Fiends"?...joyfully dig through feces. Another method of transport is…? You guessed it! "Keestering"! Aaaargh! What would we do without these folks willing to shove just about anything up there ass? At any rate; excluding these grotesque methods of transport, it might be better to enroll in the readily available Narcotics Anonymous programs most facilities offer.

JAIL 101

SMOKING

Fire the hypnotist and flush the nicotine patches. Nothing beats incarceration as a smoking cessation program. Aside from being contraband; the shape of cigarette packs, deters even the most devout "Keesterers". Enjoy the lack of "cancer sticks" and take the first steps to a smoke-less, albeit freedom-less, life!

JAIL 101

APOLOGIZING

Inevitably, while in jail, you will find yourself compelled to apologize or beg for mercy. Never say "I'm so**y". In the event that you forget this rule and say "I'm s**ry"; you will immediately be labeled a "bitch", and end up with your "end up". The statement "I apologize..." should be used sparingly, and in place of the aforementioned phrase.

JAIL 101

SELF DEFENSE

Your safety is important. Therefore levity has been spared in this section. There will be a time when you must defend yourself, a friend, or simply put, the structural integrity of your (you've attracted the attention of "Bolo the Bunghole Banger") posterior portal. The quickest way to disable an attacker is with an "eye rake". To render your nemesis sightless: Simply cross-grab their wrist with your opposite hand. Example: Your left hand grabs their left wrist. Pull on their wrist, step forward and rake, gouge, or claw, like a little girl. This is the only time it is acceptable to behave like a "little bitch". Follow up with a kick or knee to the offenders groin and find the nearest Correctional Officer or "Room Service" button.

JAIL 101

TIME MANAGEMENT

Time. Outside we never have enough. Well take heart. After your inevitable arrest and subsequent sentencing. You will have more "free time" (Poor choice of words, 'I apologize'. Note: I did not say "I'm so**y") than you know what to do with. Consider this for a moment. How many times have you said... "If I had more time I would... 'stretch more, learn a new language, write a screenplay, write a book (Case in point: As I write this, I am sitting on my bunk (top) Indian style; no hanging feet, even though I trust Jake not to "Manson" me). learn to ballroom dance, (difficult... space limitations) or read more books. F.Y.I: In Jail, you may receive books from "outside", however, they must be sent directly from a publisher or distributor, such as "Amazon". You may not have your loved ones or unincarcerated fellow felons, send you books from private collections. Authorities believe this curtails entry of coded information. 'What Fools!' Example: 'For stronger 'Madres Famous Rum Cake' add "Mas Redrum" equals "Murder Sam". As mentioned previously, incoming mail is searched and presumably read. This is challenge enough for the life forms charged with this duty. There is no way the State could afford the overtime if they were required to read books!

JAIL 101

FIFI BAG

The "Fifi Bag" is a distasteful, unnecessary, but unfortunately common item to be used only in times of unimagined, or is that "unimaginative" loneliness. The "Fifi Bag" can be purchased pre-constructed for prices ranging from 2-5 soups. Soups are available from "Commissary"; average cost $1.00 each. Alternatively, you may construct your own, using the following instructions.

1. Start by locating a sandwich size plastic or paper bag. (A larger bag will be needed if your ancestors were Italian or African. Indians and Asians may get away with an empty "Sweet n low" packet.)

2. Locate a fresh banana peel.

3. Gather up those invaluable adhesives. (Remember to keep all fruit labels, as well as diabetic and other special meal stickers.)

4. Tailor the banana peel to your phallus's circumferential measurement and use the sticky labels to secure the ends. (Moist side-skin side!)

5. Secure the banana peel inside the rim of the bag by lapping the bag slightly over the peel and fastening it with the sticky (and soon to be stickier) labels.

6. Use and discard. (Preferably in a bio-hazard receptacle)

JAIL 101

TRUMPED UP CHARGES

As you make your way through the cells of justice. You will see the same phrase scribbled and scribed on walls, benches and bunks; "Are you serious?" This phrase (if written by one person, he is a terrible criminal with a serious case of writers cramp) refers to the insane process of throwing the whole kitchen sink and all of the household cleaning supplies at the defendant. Example: You are arrested after an incident at a bar. The incident, from your perspective, occurred as follows. Some drunkard elicited a physical response from you by pushing you in the chest with both hands. As you collect yourself and apologize for spilling your beer all over your mini-skirt, tube-top clad, 5'11", copper toned, brunette "bombshell" date! You turn around and your attacker is advancing on your position with a posse' of four, who intend to thwart your evenings ambitions with an advanced ass kicking! As they close in: You, realizing you are in possession of an empty beer bottle; take the opportunity to throw the beer bottle at them in hopes of evening the odds. This is where it gets weird. The Police walk in as you are in mid launch. The bottle bounces harmlessly off of "Bolos" chest. The Police "cuff and stuff" you. You spend countless hours, cold, blue-balled, and chained to a chair. Finally, after being "booked". You are sitting in a cell with paperwork that among other things; indicates you are being charged with "Assault With A Deadly Weapon With Force Enough To Create Great Bodily Injury", a class (A) Felony that carries a 2-5 year prison sentence. "Absurd" you say? It happens everyday. This is where the phrase "plea bargaining" comes into play. You surely do not want to spend that much time waiting for another crack at the "Busty Brunette". Although girls do like "bad boys", a few days in jail, is adequate to create this persona. Your bail is $50,000; at 5-10% down (sacrificed), you decide to see if the judge will let you out on your "own recognizance" (O.R.). If you are a "real criminal" not a faker, you will have warrants in other counties and/or a yard long R.A.P. (record of arrested person) sheet, with a history of F.T.A. (failure to appear), eliminating the chance of a simple court date and release. You sit in jail and life goes on (for others), and wait for your court date. At your "Arraignment" (anti-climactic court date), the Judge views your charge(s), your outstanding warrant(s) and your historical disinterest in showing up for court (F.T.A.), and "remands" you (Throws your ass back in jail). Two to four weeks later, you show up in court, wearing "Heavy jewelry". Your Attorney says you are "screwed... cops make great witnesses... blah blah blah." You hold your breath, ponder going to trial, and try to imagine what showering with others is like. Your Attorney waits until he sees your pupils dilate, your jugular vein distend, and a fine layer of perspiration develop on your forehead. He then says, "The D.A., ("Diabolical Asshole") being the benevolent person they are, is offering a "deal". In exchange for your plea of "guilty" or "no contest" (basically the same, "no contest" just lessens the chance of civil action against you), they will modify the charge to a simple "Assault With A Deadly Weapon"; class (B) Felony; sentence = 90 days in County Jail and 3 years formal probation." Or, depending on your record; "Misdemeanor Battery"; sentence = 100 community service hours and a $500.00 fine. No group showers sounds good and you take the "deal". The D.A. keeps his conviction percentage up (the only thing he can "keep up"). Your Attorney lightens his case load. And you? You either buy incredibly expensive phone cards from "Commissary" to keep the "Brunette" warm, or put on an orange vest, and do your part to keep our highways litter-free.

JAIL ETIQUETTE

Your adherence to the following rules of conduct while incarcerated equals the difference between a peaceful jail existence and being beaten beyond recognition.

The last thing you want in jail, or life, for that matter, is a blown out anus! Regardless of the mechanism! So exercise extreme caution when choosing your friends (stay away from people with names such as "Bolo the Bunghole Banger") and pay close attention to the rules of engagement, while utilizing the following "Twist/Flush/Push" procedure.

Although neither of us has ever suffered through the catastrophic degradation or deterioration of our "Master O-ring", we've seen it. No! Strike that! We have heard someone suffering through the heinous process of O-ring recalibration. At any rate. Any way you look at it, it's not pretty. Let's move on!

The "Twist/Flush/Push" procedure is simply put. "A way to conceal and dispose of auditory and physical bowel emissions."

It would be a massive understatement to say, "Jail plumbing is high powered". The vacuum created by these institutional toilets has been known to suck in testicles to the point of castration. We are quite confident; we could flush a fully inflated basketball down the pipe of our cell toilet. Picture a commercial aircraft toilet on steroids or similarly, a catastrophic cabin decompression of said aircraft, at 35,000 feet, in 4.356 seconds, through a fist sized orifice. As Criminals concerned with etiquette. These obscenely loud and overpowered "thrones" are just another modern institutional blessing.

NOTE: The average modern jail toilet flushes and fills in 4.356 seconds.

Start the process by having your cellmate assume the "fecal position". This position entails lying on their side, face to the wall, with a blanket over their head. Their legs should be drawn up to a 1/2 bent position for maximum comfort, they may be there for a while.

Once seated on the stainless steel "throne", become familiar with your surroundings. Practice placing your finger or hand on the flush button or handle. This contortion may take some time and proper alignment of your spine. Sit up straight! Now relax! Let Mother Nature and your physiology chart a mutual fecal course. Let it build! Note: This brings up a key point; always eat whatever fiber is available to you in jail. Any lapse in fiber intake will result in a complete breakdown of this procedure. When confidence in complete expulsion is high: Twist, Flush, and Push with maximal intent to transfer all colonic contents into the growling receptacle, within the 4.356 second time frame. Use caution, not to strain, thereby preserving the structural integrity of your master O-ring. Repeat as necessary.

JAIL 101

PROFANITY

The role of a Correctional Officer is very taxing. In between naps and snacks, they have a daily quota of profanity to fulfill. After close analysis; we can only deduce that they suspect everyone, including their co-workers, of having sex with their Mothers, for they constantly refer to everyone as "Motherfuckers". This off-color vocabulary, sadly, rubs off on the Inmate population. Prepare yourself by mimicking someone with advanced Turrets Syndrome for easier assimilation and/or acceptance.

JAIL 101

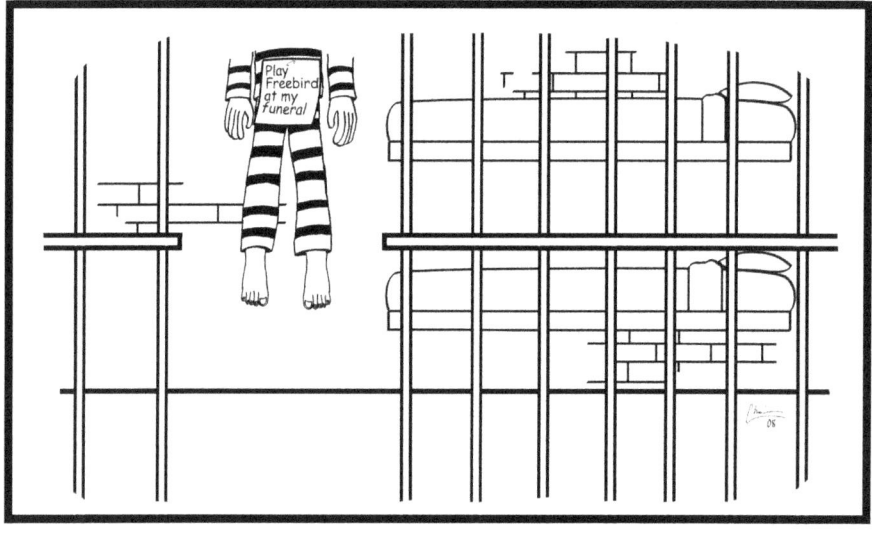

SUICIDE

There are few greater reasons for suicide, than the prospect of spending ones remaining years, behind bars. Exhaust all hope of overturning the verdict in Appeals Court and spend gross amounts of time planning, and hopefully achieving escape (see "Techno-gopher"), before taking the express train to meet your maker. Save a tree, no note is necessary, lifetime incarceration is self explanatory.

JAIL 101

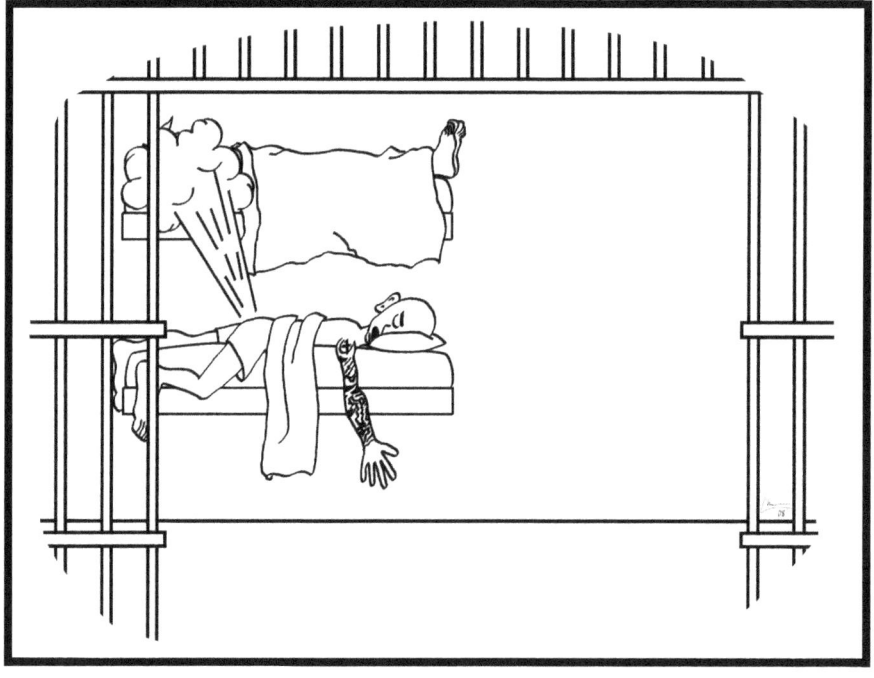

BUNKS

Basic physics should be taken into account when given the choice between a top or bottom bunk. Pay special attention to gas laws (hot air rises). Jail bunks are narrow, so fitful sleepers (law of gravity) should request or fight for lower elevation accommodations. Note: Modern facilities scoff at fitted sheets and do not issue pillows; so tie your sheets at the corners, and use books, shoes, latex gloves, and imagination, to create a headrest.

JAIL 101

TOILET USE

If you are a demonstrative defecater, you have found Mecca. However, do not expect your peers to appreciate your flamboyant voiding. If you are modest, try covering yourself with a sheet. (Preferably not a white sheet, for there are many African Americans in jail, who may misinterpret your need for privacy.) Don't worry if you forget to "courtesy flush"; some better mannered "Motherfucker" will remind you.

JAIL 101

QUEST FOR FIRE

Modern advances have solved the "Quest for fire". However, punitive institutions, much like Quakers, deprive their constituents of modern ignition devices; such as lighters, matches, butane torches, etc. To disregard alignment with this conservative mentality, improvise as follows: Step 1. Remove the lead from a pencil. Step 2. Place the lead between the prongs of an appliance cord, such as a TV, radio charger, "hotpot", etc. Step 3. Tie a 6 inch strand of toilet paper around the middle of the lead shaft. Step 4. Slowly plug the prongs into an electrical outlet. This will cause a direct short, a subsequent flame, and ignite the paper. Use Caution: Correctional Officers are not fans of creativity.

JAIL 101

JAIL LINGO

Understanding and possessing a solid command of lingo exclusive to jail is not only cool and allows one to appear as a dyed in the wool veteran, it is also just plain fun! "Jay cat", a frequently heard term, describes a prisoner who doesn't play well with others, e.g., "snitches", "bitches", eats other folks food, or engages in other inappropriate or enigmatic behavior. Being labeled a "Jay cat" is degrading at best and may be life threatening, blend in! "Feel me"; defined as, "Can you relate or do you understand?" Is a term exclusive to the African American tribe and is NOT an invitation to fondle. (If you are not black and use this term, under any circumstances, the creator of this book, prays you are labeled a "Jay cat" and severely beaten!) "Roll it up" A phrase commanding you to gather your things and roll up your bedroll, was formerly, exclusively used by Correctional Officers. It typically implied you were destined for release or transfer, and had positive connotations. (Unless the transfer was to a less desirable location, such as, moving in with "Bolo the Bunghole Banger") In recent times, like all good things, "Roll it up" has been tainted, and may be interpreted, when emitted from the "cakehole" of another Inmate, as "Get the fuck outta here!" "Man walking" is a phrase describing the arrival or presence of a Correctional Officer. Failure to alert other Inmates to the presence of a C.O., and thus alleviating them of ample time to conceal contraband, is considered poor form.

JAIL 101

COMMISSARY

Christmas comes once a week in jail, providing you have been nice to someone capable of putting "$$ on your books"; a Prisoner account maintained by the facility, from which you may draw. Items available from "Commissary" include; toothbrushes, tuna, chili, candy, stamps, shoes, phone cards, coffee, etc. Note: Unless you are a frequent attendee, the process may take a few weeks. To begin: Ask a friend or loved one to send money in the preferred form of the facility. Once received, the facility will credit the funds to your account and you will be on your way to a more lavish jail existence. "Indigent items", for Inmates with "no love outside", although sparse, are available.

SNITCHING

"Loose lips sink ships", and nobody likes a "tattletale", especially criminals. Inmates have good memories and generous amounts of time to plot revenge. Unless you have a death wish or enjoy high anxiety living, "Keep your mouth shut!"

JAIL 101

GANGS

Gangs are good. They allow one to feel safe and cared for. Most facilities go to great lengths to honor affiliation and avoid violence, through segregation. Race and geographics typically determine a Prisoner's partisanship. For example: You will rarely see an African American "rolling" with the Hispanic element. African Americans wearing red are "Bloods"; those wearing blue are "Crips". At times of peace, rival gang members may fraternize. However, when "shit pops off", that is; violence is imminent or taking place. Gangs re-group, cast off congeniality and take necessary action determined by their individual hierarchies. Hispanic gangs fall into two basic categories; "Norteno's" and "Sureno's". "Norteno's sport four dot tattoos and associate themselves with the number "14". "Sureno's" sport three dots and associate themselves with number "13". Most Asians fall under the heading "Chino's". Caucasians "roll" with the "Woods" (short for "Peckerwoods"). "Pacific Islanders" consist of Hawaiians, Filipinos, Samoans, Tongans, etc. Uninterested or different Prisoners are categorized as "Others".

THINGS TO KNOW WHEN YOU GO

SPORK

A modern institutional marvel that surpasses all other utensils in efficiency. This combination fork and spoon made of high grade plastic, is not just the only culinary implement you need in jail, it is the only one you get! Careful! As you become progressively more enamored by its utilitarian prowess, you may find yourself (after your release? or escape?), prowling fast food restaurants, searching for what will surely be, an inadequate substitute. Caution: Never misplace, loan, or lose, your "Spork"!

JAIL 101

ADDRESS CONCEALMENT

Jail is a good place to be paranoid. You would have to travel far and wide, or wait... to the local D.A.'s office, to surround yourself with a more unscrupulous crowd. Bearing in mind your close quartered, morally compromised, fellow inmates. It is good practice to conceal your address and limit the dissemination of other personal information. It's difficult enough to sleep in jail, without the thought of the location of your home, loved ones, or other belongings, being available to criminals "Outside". Always tear off, punch out, throw away, and/or flush addresses printed on mail or court documents.

JAIL 101

H₂O THROUGH A DOOR

If you slept through physics or were too busy preparing for your career as a criminal. Fret no more! Jail is full of physics lessons. We touched on gravity and gas laws in the "Bunks" section. Here; we will provide you with a formula for pouring H2O through a door, using guess what... physics! In Jail, "Inside", hot water has the value of gold, "Outside". During "lockdown" (naptime or playtime for Correctional Officers and occasionally post violence within the facility). The "Hotpot", always tethered by heavy chains, for obvious reasons, will be inaccessible. Often, the "Trustees" will be the only Prisoners uncaged. Although Correctional Institutions grant "Trustees" above average Prisoner liberties, they stop short of giving them keys. If given permission, the "Trustees" will likely distribute "hot water" during troubled times, to those equipped for reception. This blessed fluid is used for soup, coffee, tea, etc., available from "Commissary". The following instructions will allow you to be a grateful and highly acclaimed recipient. Start by locating an intact medium size bag; such as an empty 6 oz. potato chip bag, available from Commissary. Rinse the bag thoroughly and rip a bottom corner off. Next: Slide the top of the bag through the door jam and place the corner in your cup. Let physics (water always seeks the path of least resistance) do the rest, as the coveted fluid fills your cup. Always say "Thank you"!

JAIL 101

CHOWTIMES

Unorthodox meal times in Jail are a violation of ones circadian rhythm. However, minus any additional subsistence from "Commissary", you will acclimate quickly to eating breakfast, well before the "cock crows". Lunch, another oddly timed meal, is served well before midday, and dinner arrives at the time most kids are having after school milk and cookies. Alarm clocks are unnecessary! The burden of early rising is easily overcome by a starvation inducing twelve hour gap between dinner and breakfast.

JAIL 101

HYGIENE

Proper hygiene benefits your morale and is a precursor to enhanced public relations. Shave and shower daily to promote feelings of well-being and freshness. Trim finger and toe nails to avoid the collection of bacteria and/or germs. The only reluctance to following these recommendations should be a need for a disgusting appearance, foul smell, and long finger nails, to repel admirers such as, 'you guessed it!'... "Bolo the Bunghole Banger"!

JAIL 101

GRIEVANCE FORMS

Everybody has a grievance in jail: "My Attorney is an idiot". "That Judge is a racist". "My cellmate shakes the bunk all night, like a pre-pubescent girl with a new hula hoop!" These grievances can all be dealt with. Some involve paperwork. Example: You can always request or obtain new Counsel. Some require physical action. Example: A finely tuned "Sporking" to the groin of your cellmate, should stifle those nightly tremors and motivate them into a voluntary "roll up". At times you may feel inclined to tattle on a Correctional Officer or Deputy for mistreating or abusing you, in the form of a "Grievance form". This is similar to filing a 'Citizens Complaint" against a Cop, and then moving in with them! Never do it! Period! Alternatively, contact "Outside" assistance, and have them assault the Institution and the Governor, with a barrage of letters. I personally would like to see a website, with the names, addresses, and Inmate abuse records, of Correctional Officers! Go webmasters!

JAIL 101

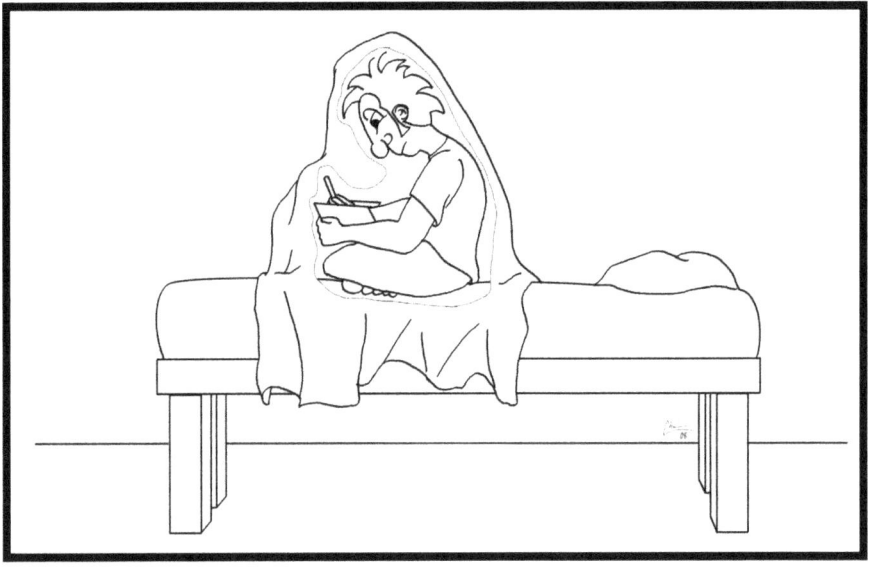

JOURNALS

Journals are therapeutic; regardless of how "gay" you look when writing in one. (You may want to burn this historical account of your incarceration, upon release or escape) However, it does not hurt to process on paper, the daily delights of Jail. And besides, it is always better to write about "Sporking" your cellmate to death, than to break your "Spork" in the process. The following entry from my journal is about "nicknaming" fellow felons. Feel free to follow suit and "nickname" yours.

Another day in an 8x10. Jake just returned from "pill call". He said, "You look scary looking out that window from out there." Does a Tiger look happy in a cage? Have you been to the Zoo and watched the Tigers pace? Do you think they would tear you up, if released at that moment? Our six inch wide cell door window, a.k.a., the "Wicked Window" is a portal to a place I don't want to be, but a place better than where I am. I nickname the top tier inmates. There is "Cro-Magnum", an excessively hairy felon, in here on gun charges. He drinks tea and has a peculiar appreciation for the exhausted tea bag. He always places it in his mouth, draws the juice out, rips it open with his teeth, and munches on the contents. I've never tried this. It seems like it would have an odd texture—it works for him. "Cardiovascular Man" just left, released. He had recently undergone a quadruple bypass. I don't talk to these people. Jake talks to them during his tri-daily trips to the Nurse for medications. Jake takes insulin: A shot in the stomach, twice a day, along with a psych med and a long lasting oral dose of insulin in the evening. He has the scoop on these people and we nickname them as they pass by our "Wicked Window". What do they think of me? I walk fast laps each morning, coffee cup in hand. Sometimes I hear snickering. Once I heard someone call me "The Machine". My routine is predictable. I guess I am "The Machine". I walk in the morning and go outside in the afternoon from 1-2 pm, to the rec. area. I either do pull-ups or dips, alternating each day, like clockwork. I mix in abdominal exercises and sunbathing, my pants rolled up, socks off, shirtless, standing on my sandals between sets. I shoot baskets as well. Although, I am only effective at long range "hook shots". People howl when I make one, a short lived thrill. "Cardiovascular Man" does laps, just like me. Once I encouraged him, as he passed by my cell. "Good work man", I barked through my door. He gave me a thumbs up and continued. He came by and introduced himself an hour before his release. His name was David, and I was alarmed when he spoke, his humanness revealed. He encouraged me to keep walking. He said he watches me everyday. I felt ashamed for denying his identity, as a person. To me, he had always been an image to mock, in hopes of eliciting a chuckle from Jake. Actually, I take that back. I never mocked him. Just things like "Wow 'Cardiovascular Man' is fast today." The "Wicked Window" never lets you out there. We just watch them. It's a "Circular Aquarium" of swimming criminals. "Bob Zombie" is scary. He circles, scowling, jaw and hands clenching. He stops and stares at things only he sees, projecting disdain. He moves slow. Jake found out that "Bob Zombie" is here because he beat someone over the head with a pipe. It had to of been pre-meditated, he moves to slow for spontaneity. "John Travolta" just rolled up onto the set, his hair feathered perfectly. "Barry Bonds", just left, released. He called "Cardiovascular man", "Speedy". Jake found that out in the "Pill-call" line. I guess we are not the only Inmates who nickname "them", when looking out the "Wicked Window".

JAIL 101

ROUTINES

Correctional facility staff are sticklers for routine and frown, heavy-handedly, on spontaneity. So, as the saying goes... "If you can't beat 'em... (and trust me, you can't!)... join 'em." In addition to taking advantage of more "Free time", ("I apologize" Note: I did not say "I'm so**y") as mentioned in the "Time Management" section. It is also beneficial to integrate routines based on the scheduling parameters of the institution, thereby, allowing your sentenced time to pass in a most succinct fashion. Take the routine described below, (my current routine) as a prototype, and prepare yourself.

At 3:30 a.m. the door lock on our cell door "Pops" (unlocks). This "Pop" is the signal for breakfast. Consider this word for a moment. "Break-fast". No where is this word more poignant, than in jail, where (barring any "Commissary") everyday, from 3:45 p.m. to 3:45 a.m., one engages in involuntary fasting. This unprecedented daily caloric deprivation, means, that even if I am deeply sleeping in horizontal heaven on top of Pamela Anderson. This "Pop" inspires me to a vertical position in haste that would make "Pavlov", salivate, rollover, bark, and urinate all over the kitchen linoleum! After inhaling the 670 calorie "Fastbreaker", I read or write, (although excessive literacy is frowned upon and I run the risk of being labeled a "Jay cat") while others emit gross quantities of "Methane" and shout homicidal threats in their sleep. Depending on the intensity of the literature and/or amount of toxic fumes, I stay awake until the 8:00 a.m. "Pop" or pass out.

At 8:00 a.m., the door "Pops" again, signifying "Program" Time. This equates to one hour out of the less than luxurious confines of my 8'x10', cinderblock and steel "House". A "House" equipped with generous, yet control-

JAIL 101

lable, white fluorescent lighting and a "HIGH-POWER" combination, stainless steel toilet/sink. The designers were also sadistic enough to include; one can only assume, in the interest of preventing easy slumber and increasing the likelihood of a homicide, a red light in the overhead fluorescent assembly, that never, ever, goes off!

The 8-9:00 a.m. exterior "pod" hour, a.k.a. "Circular Aquarium", is a time for me to caffeinate and walk laps, while being subjected to scrutiny, ridicule, name-calling and nick-naming by inmates still confined on the top tier, as they peer with malice out their "Wicked Windows". A good time for all!

From 9-10:00 a.m. I, among other activities and continued caffeination, stare out my "Wicked Window" and watch the top tier inmates engage in "Circular Aquarium". I regain my self respect by scrutinizing, ridiculing, name calling, and nick-naming! A good time for all!

10:30 a.m. brings another "Pop" and we form a single file line of inmates in hypoglycemic stupors, eager to lay hands on our 670 calorie lunch. After inhaling lunch, I typically do a Twist/Flush/Push procedure (Jake assumes the "Fecal Position") and resign myself to "R&R", that is… "reading and resting".

A "Pop" at 1:00 p.m., sends me scurrying to the attached 20'x20' Recreation Area. This heavily fortified "dawg kennel" is equipped with a pull-up/dip bar apparatus and basketball hoop. I attack the pull-up/dip bar apparatus with the fervor of a "one legged man in an ass kicking contest" and shoot hoops for one hour. The tall concrete walls and "maximum security" steel grate ceiling, (even the ball cannot escape!) also doubles as an excellent handball court. At 2:00 pm we are "locked down", and depending on the availability of extra calories from "Commissary", I attack my illegal exercise chart drawn on the 'concrete canvas' cell wall. This chart is comprised of 21 physical activities ranging from running in place, martial arts forms and kicks, wall squats, push-ups, sit-ups, "burpies", lunges, stretching, etc., while Jake sleeps.

3:30 p.m. brings another "Pop" and its dinner time. We once again form a single file line and circle the perimeter of the "pod" to the "Chow" tray dispensing "Trustees". After receiving my tray, I retreat to my cell to quell the starvation, in a nick of time.

From 3:45 p.m. to 8:00 p.m., I rest, read, write, (Jake sleeps) or try to look through thick netting, at the female prisoners, in their "Yard". All the while enduring the male prisoners above me, incessantly banging on their 4" windows, in attempts to solicit mammary shots. A good time for all!

The 8:00 p.m. "Pop" signifies another "program" hour. Among other things, I discuss upcoming gang violence, scare people, exchange contraband, drink some coffee, take a shower, use the phone and engage in general mayhem. A good time for all!

At 9:00 p.m. we are "locked down". I read, write letters, discuss a myriad of topics with Jake, (most of which revolve around the female anatomy) say my prayers, and go to sleep. Another day down!

JAIL 101

CREDIT FOR TIME SERVED

There are advantages to being a well behaved criminal. "Credit for time served" calculations, vary from County to County, Check with yours to determine if you should refrain from "Spork" evisceration of that repeat "Methane" offender.

Let's take Santa Clara County (our current location) as an example. In Santa Clara County, one receives "Good time" credit. This "good-time", (what an oxymoron!!) equates to (CTS) "credit for time served". The (ATS) "Actual time served" is, as it sounds, the actual time you have spent in custody. "Credit for time served" in Santa Clara County for example, equates to you doing, roughly, two thirds of your sentence. Example: Your Sentence is 6 months: Barring any misconduct or the inability to play nice with others, you would serve 4 months (ATS) and get credit for 6 months (CTS). Unfortunately, even model Prisoners may be "caught up" in a riot, fight, contraband smuggling operation, etc., in which they truly did not participate. This bogus "guilt by proximity" often leads to a loss of "good time" and additional charges. Therefore, if you have foreknowledge of an impending riot or fight. Latch on, like a friendly remora, to the nearest Correctional Officer and ride it out. This will help you to avoid additional time, but may get you killed. It's a "dicey" situation, be forewarned!

JAIL 101

VISITS

Jail visits are complex. Depending on where you are, they can be as impersonal as talking on a phone separated by thick glass. Or, at the State Prison level, weekend long, with double-wide trailer accommodations, allowing the production of future Felons. Whatever the type. They are typically uplifting and encouraged. All visitors must go through a metal detector. We recommend they arrive early, have a Dr.'s note for that steel plate in their head, and never wear a bra! (They have wire in them! Hee! Hee!)

JAILHOUSE LAWYERS

You've heard the term, "Everybody is innocent in Jail." It's not true! Many inmates take pride in their crimes and the details get more colorful as time goes on. "...and then I took that pigs gun away, held it to his head and said "gimme my doo rag back! Feel me!" Many of these super criminals also maintain they have vast and superior knowledge of your charge(s) and profound legal expertise that might compel you to fire Johnny Cochran's nephew. Each case is different and your personal history factors largely into your future place of residence. With this in mind. Listen to what they have to say, but don't enter a plea based on your "pod posse" of Attorneys. Instead, compare notes with a licensed professional.

JAIL 101

RELIGION

Do you believe in a higher power such as Jesus? Allah? Shiva? Neptune? In Jail, while the cuisine takes it toll, you can save your soul. ("Man cannot live by bread alone") Aside from getting you out of your cell; studying theology is a positive experience, in a negative place. Also, one should consider the possibility that a deficient value set, may be what landed you smack in the middle of all of this concrete and steel. With time to kill, why not spend some of it exploring a new or refreshing an old philosophical slant? Maybe you can't ride that "Magic Carpet" to freedom, but a little "soul food" never hurt.

JAIL 101

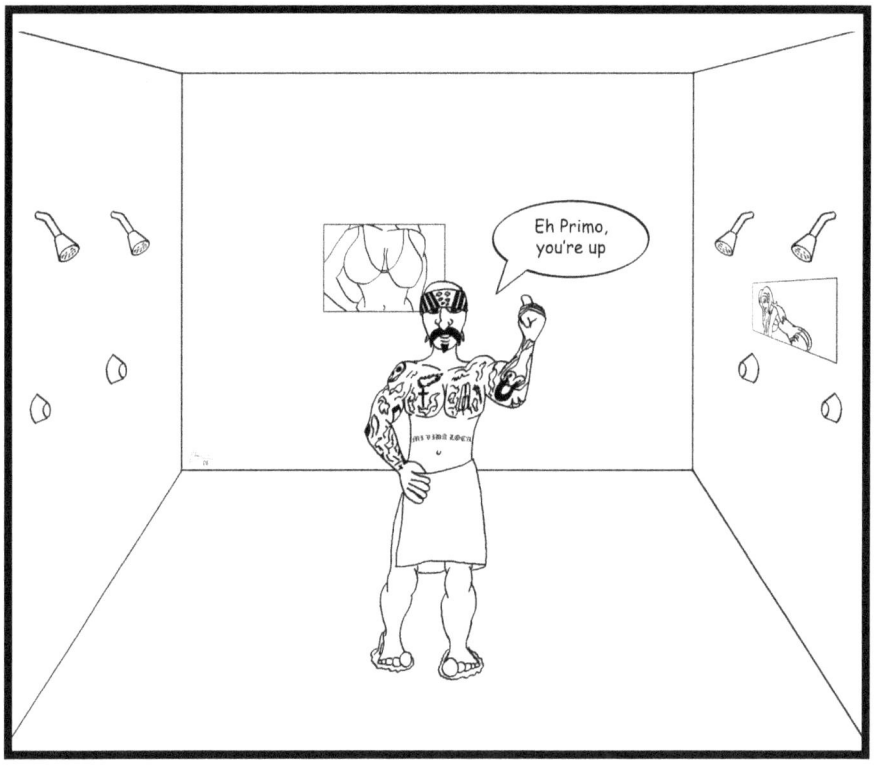

SHOWER SHOTS

You might consider wrapping your Government Issue "shower shoes'" in plastic, before wading your way through "man goo", to this visual-aid. Plastered porn, a.k.a., a "Shower Shot", is a symbol of how far mankind can slide, when anointing the walls of jail shower stalls.

JAIL 101

LATEX PILLOWS

In jail, just like "Outside". It's not what you know, it's who you know. In Jail, the people to know are the "Trustees". These "Masters of the Mansion' are the people to turn to, when you need "something special". Whether it is a new toothbrush, an extra blanket. Hot water during "lockdowns", a "shower shot", sugar or yeast for "pruno, the thermostat turned up in the "Cold room". Note: The "Cold Room" is a holding cell used to house Inmates who have done something, or sometimes nothing, to raise the ire of the Correctional Staff. The room is intentionally "bone-chilling" and any complaints result in the removal of clothing; if you had any to begin with, and the lowering of the thermostat. It is mystfying to me, that this common practice, is allowed in the year 2010. 'Hello? ACLU? Is anybody home?' Among the "Trustees" duties, are serving the food and cleaning the showers, sometimes in the same hour. This multi-tasking results in a justifiable concern for hygiene. Therefore, they are well stocked with latex gloves.

To create a Latex Pillow: Follow these instructions:

1. Acquire a minimum of six latex gloves. More is better!

2. Tie the ends of the fingers together, 3 gloves to 3 gloves, or more.

3. Inflate the gloves with lung power and tie.

4. Say your prayers!

5. Sleep well.

PARDONS AND PROGRAMS

Sometime during your incarceration, you may feel inclined to request a pardon or suggest a program to the Governor. The Governor is a busy man, so keep it short and to the point. The following sample letter was submitted in regards to a program we wholeheartedly believe, would be incredibly beneficial to Inmates and society overall.

JAIL 101

Dear Governor Schwarzenegger: (That still makes me laugh, even when I write it !)

As qualified experts of contemporary Correctional Facilities, we share a conviction to help inmates and society through progressive inmate reform programs. We strongly believe that the following program would be a fresh and firm instrument in mankind's Penal code violator reform process. Please apply the necessary thrust to implement this program without pause. The following are details of the P.S.P. submitted for your close inspection. Please have your aides closely scrutinize our plan and bring any holes to our attention, AS SOON AS POSSIBLE!

Your constituents at California Correctional Facilities share the common knowledge that most offenses or actions committed against the grain or fabric of modern societal government are the by-product of an unrelenting drive for MORE PUSSY! Therefore, we firmly believe, the PUSSY SATURATION PROGRAM (P.S.P.) would alleviate building pressures in Correctional facilities, as well as benefit ex-cons and society, long after the Inmate's release. Your quick action is requested is disseminating the necessary funds for gross pussy acquisition and dispersement throughout Statewide Correctional Facilities.

In closing, because the details are a little fuzzy; with all humility, we recommend you appoint a group of qualified analysts, including ourselves, to head this program. Thank you for your close consideration. Please send all questions, comments, or prototypes, to:

Santa Clara County Department of Correction
Main Jail C/O Friedman Newman/ BVR867
885 N. San Pedro st. POD 7A Cell # 9
San Jose, Ca. 95110

JAIL 101

JAIL DENTISTRY

Have you been putting off that wisdom tooth extraction because of scheduling or expense? Procrastinate no more! When you go to jail, your calendar is instantly cleared and you can forget about writing that rubber check. Nobody does a better extraction than a Jail Dentist. "Why are they so adept?" you ask, with "baited" breath. Because that's ALL THEY DO! You have two options regarding dental issues in jail. 1. Endure the pain 2. Lose the tooth. We recommend the former if at all possible. Having a criminal record is bad. Having a criminal record and being toothless is worse. Caution: Never mix Acetaminophen with "Pruno". Ibuprofen is available through "Commissary".

JAIL 101

SIMPLE FLATULENCE

In 2 man, 8'x10' cells; common in modern "Pod" style Correctional Facilities, (I am sitting in one, as I write this) you will find two vents. The incoming air is the "supply" and the exiting air is the "return". Simple logic allows one to determine, that in the interest of maintaining tolerable air quality, it would be most advantageous to post oneself as proximal as possible to the "return", prior to emitting any "methane". Observance of this simple procedure will offer cellmates a better chance of peaceful long-term coexistence.

JAIL 101

CONDUCT

Take it from us. Going bare toe to steel toe with your captors is never a good idea. Jake recently witnessed an Inmate punch a Correctional Officer in the face, knocking him unconscious. The Inmate expired 4 days later as a result of the blunt trauma and associated skull fractures secondary to being beaten by many "men with large flashlights". In addition to keeping your hands to yourself, it is wise to hold ones tongue. I once inquired as to the motive for locking us down. The answer was, "we are short staffed". I couldn't help myself. I replied, "I know you have small dicks, but why are you locking us down." They didn't see the humor in my response and' 'Why did I say that?' was my last complete thought, before hypothermia set in.

Sadly but truly, prisoners are often subjected to excessive and unwarranted physical attention. Case in point: Once, while wearing "heavy jewelry" in a holding cell. I was minding my own business, lost in thoughts of bail amounts and sentences, when I was shaken from my reverie, by a Police Officer opening the cell door. He summoned me, and I approached, anticipating transfer, or a chance to phone home. The Officer, assuming I had my guard down, let go with a vicious kick aimed at my testicles.(I shudder to think, what this guys dog looks like) I prize my jewels and rotated my hips, causing him to miss, by an inch, as he quickly slammed the steel door. This upset me to the point of performing aggressive stress testing of said door. The door was failing and I was on my way out to show "Officer Fascist" how a man, not a "bitch", like himself, kicks. When he and his friends ("pack mentality of the insecure") entered my cell and subdued me with a bit of the "Ultra Violence".

Jake has also been the unlucky recipient of "goon squad" justice. Some time before I moved in; Jake, an insulin dependent diabetic, was deprived of his snack; an extra meal diabetics receive, to counteract the sugar see-saw of insulin administration. He could not see or stand and had to crawl to the "Room Service" button. The "handlers" arrived and told him to stand up. After listening to his excuse for intruding on their "playstation time". They handcuffed and dragged him (his shoulder is still torn up) out of the "pod" and down the hallway. For good measure, while the "men with large flashlights" dragged him, their female mascot kneed him in the ribs and back. After depositing him in the "cold room". They, not satisfied, smashed his head and face into the wood bench and left him lying there, still sugar free. Thankfully, the Nurse returned from her break, in a nick of time, and verified his medical condition. His less than congenial keepers aroused him and inspired him to eat, by bashing him about the head and shoulders with a brown box lunch. Shame on him for having a medical emergency.

JAIL 101

HANGING FEET

Ankles, like wrists, make great handles. However, "grab your ankles!" is not a phrase you want to hear in jail, unless... lets move on! Likewise, you do not want anyone else grabbing your ankles. Keeping this in mind; never hang your feet off the top bunk. It is rude! The Inmate below you does not want to view or smell your "hooves" (hopefully) anymore, than you want to view or smell theirs. Something else to consider, is the omnipresent threat of your lower level "bunkie" going "Manson", and indulging himself, by watching your cerebral spinal fluid gush out; as you lie unconscious on the concrete cell floor.

JAIL CUISINE

If you haven't taken pre-emptive measures regarding the placement of "Money on your books" (see "Commissary") at your pre-destined place of incarceration. Do not delay! Still don't believe us? Take a sniff of this weekly menu. This should be all the motivation you need to dig out your old "Piggy Bank", or someone else's.

Monday	Tuesday	Wednesday
<u>Breakfast</u>	<u>Breakfast</u>	<u>Breakfast</u>
Corn flakes.	Grits, milk,	Shit on shingle S.O.S.
Slice of cold bologna	1 cup fake eggs	(We have no idea what this is!)
Milk	tiny slice of sugar cake	
Tiny plain donut		
<u>Lunch</u>	<u>Lunch</u>	<u>Lunch</u>
1 roll, 1 cheese slice orange, milk	cheese sandwich, milk orange	salami sandwich milk, apple
<u>Dinner</u>	<u>Dinner</u>	<u>Dinner</u>
Tiny burrito	Burnt pizza	Turkey rice, brownie
½ cup corn, apple, milk	½ cup salad, milk	milk

JAIL 101

Thursday	Friday	Saturday
Breakfast	**Breakfast**	**Breakfast**
Oatmeal	corn flakes. Milk	oatmeal, fried bologna
1 cup fake eggs	bologna slice	milk
Lunch	**Lunch**	**Lunch**
Fried bologna, milk Mystery Vege's?	"cat" food, milk Apple	Ham sandwich milk Orange
Dinner	**Dinner**	**Dinner**
Fake ribs, rice	Sloppy Joe, slice of "bad" cake	"Starfish"? rice, carrots
Fruit cup, milk		

Sunday

Breakfast

corn flakes, milk, bologna slice
milk, orange

Lunch

Cat food, milk, orange

Dinner

Hotdog/bean surprise and milk

JAIL 101

THINGS TO KNOW WHEN YOU GO

JAIL JUICE

Barring incarceration during the death of a loved one or the birth of your child. Nothing is worse than ringing in the holidays behind bars. But take heart! Although you will be minus the mistletoe (hopefully!) and the rum cake. Thanks to some creative cell chemistry, you will not miss a "blasted" beat. Just be careful with this high powered contraband or you might end up with a beating for imbibing.

Follow these instructions and your "Jail juice" or "Pruno" will be ready in 6-10 days:

1. Acquire a big plastic bag. See your "Trustee" or use a "Commissary" bag.

2. Acquire fruit: Apples, Oranges, Pears, Nectarines, Ketchup, etc.

3. Smash, squash, chop and/or mutilate the fruit. Place in bag.

4. Add 2 cups sugar. See "Trustee" for kitchen contact or substitute candy from "Commissary".

5. Add $\frac{1}{2}$ tsp. yeast. See "Trustee" or toss in bread from your lunch.

6. Mix contents and tie bag tight. Apply heat. This gets tricky, be creative. Example: Fill sandwich bags with hot water from your cell sink, or retrieve hot water from the "hotpot" in your "pod" or dorm.

7. Place the hot water bag(s) or heat source snugly around the stash...beware of shakedowns. Flush immediately at first sign of "goon squad".
8. "Burp the bag" (release accumulated gases) and add sugar every 1-3 days. Beware of prying eyes and noses. Untie and hold the bag near the air "return" vent...re-tie and re-secure.

9. Drink responsibly?

KNOW THY CAPTORS

In 1971; Phillip Zombardo, and a few colleagues, performed a mock Prison experiment at Stanford University. The experiment was conducted under intense supervision and the Prisoner and Guard populations were comprised of Stanford students. Prior to being chosen, all of the students were subjected to rigorous psychological tests and were deemed sane and well adjusted. Students were only informed of the role they would be playing after signing onto the experiment. The experiment was scheduled to last two weeks. The experiment had to be terminated after six days. The Guards, consumed by their authoritarian roles, had become progressively more abusive and to the amazement of the Psychologists, violated many pre-set rules of conduct. However, the Guards were never "tardy" when scheduled, never complained about overtime, and were deeply disappointed when the experiment was shutdown. Many of the Prisoners were mentally scarred. Bear in mind that these were people who had NOT filled out a Correctional Officer employment application. These were people who had (presumably) NOT had sand kicked in their faces or been chronic bed-wetters. These were people who did NOT believe that the World Wrestling Federation is actual combat. These WERE people receiving a liberal education at one of the more esteemed Universities on planet Earth. These were NOT people whose daily dialogue consists of 95% profanity and 5% "I'm hungry". Would it be too much to suggest greater psycho-analysis of future Correctional Officers? Or perhaps like jury duty, we should all take a turn slamming doors and rattling keys. Whatever the future holds for this Profession, we can be assured that regardless of ones nurturing nature; even Ghandi left unchecked, would've morphed into a ball busting bruiser.

Have a nice stay!

STRONGER EACH DAY

Let your spirit soar above these walls. Lift your chin and let the sun wash and bathe you, as a symbol of your ever-present connection with your earth. Adjust your attitude, reclaim your dignity, and focus on the positive prospects that a new dawn presents. Education, self enrichment, and self expression are your allies even in the darkest hours. See with new eyes, the possibilities for change; not only for yourself, but for your fellow man. Consider the meeting of new cellmate as an opportunity to learn and teach. We all have shortcomings and fall short of perfection. Yet, we can all be better than the day before. Prepare yourself for finer times within these walls, and God willing, outside someday. Never lose hope and never give up. Be as a Mountain; strong each day, showered in light and immovable in your intentions.

F. Newman

Friedman Newman was born in Santa Cruz, Ca., on a moonless night. The spawn of career criminals; his Father gave him a handcuff key on his 16th birthday. Having spent much of his life behind bars, he is now almost reformed. He lives in San Francisco, Ca., with his two Black Labrador Retrievers, "Bandit" and "Smuggles".

www.ingramcontent.com/pod-product-compliance
Lightning Source LLC
Chambersburg PA
CBHW060836050426
42453CB00008B/718